Social Skills

Top 10 Mistakes That

Destroy Your Charisma...

and How to Avoid Them

I0146723

By

Stuart Killan

entertainment purposes only. All effort has been executed to present accurate, up to date, and reliable, complete information. No warranties of any kind are declared or implied. Readers acknowledge that the author is not engaging in the rendering of legal, financial, medical or professional advice. The content within this book has been derived from various sources. Please consult a licensed professional before attempting any techniques outlined in this book.

By reading this document, the reader agrees that under no circumstances is the author responsible for any losses, direct or indirect, which are incurred as a result of the use of information contained within this document, including, but not limited to, — errors, omissions, or inaccuracies.

Table Of Contents

Your Free Gift

Introduction

Chapter One: What is Charisma?

How to be Charismatic

Traits of a Charismatic Person
  Self-Confidence
  Being Optimistic
  An Emotional Player
  Being Interested and Interesting
  Demonstrating and Being Intelligent
  Being Assertive
  Maintaining Attention to Detail

Chapter Two: How do People Destroy their Charisma?

Never Introducing Themselves

Not Introducing Your Friends or Guests

Talking about Things that People do not Care About

Never Taking Feedback

Judging Others

Mumbling

Giving One-Word Answers

Whining or Complaining

Never Remembering Names

Lacking Ideas and Principles

Chapter Three: How to Improve Charisma

Always be Present in Any Conversation

Lighten Your Load

Make them Feel Like a Star

Other Tips

Use Metaphors

Use Anecdotes and Stories

Moral Conviction

Express Shared Feelings

Make Your Presence Known

Conclusion

Your Free Gift

As a way of saying thank you for downloading. I'm offering a free bonus report called *7 Habits of Highly Confident People* that's exclusive to the readers of this book.

Get instant access at http://freeconfidencebook.com

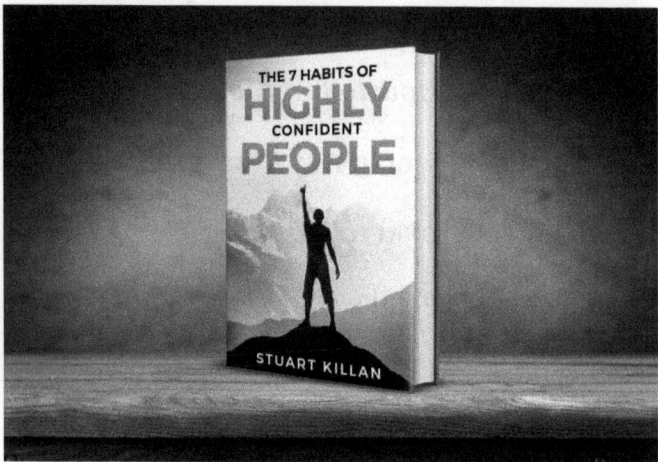

Inside the book you'll discover

- Secrets of The Joker, and why he should be admired
- The one thing confident people *always* do first when confronted with a tough situation – learning this alone can 10X your self esteem
- How to use vision boards to achieve your goals
- Identifying your "hidden talents" – even if you don't think you have any

- The one trait you must MURDER if you are to become successful
- How to never doubt your own abilities again
- Michael Jordan's #1 success secret
- The 4 most dangerous words in your vocabulary (if you're saying these regularly you are killing your own confidence)
- How to succeed as an introvert in an extrovert's world

Download for free at http://freeconfidencebook.com

Introduction

I want to thank you for choosing this book, *'Shyness: Top 10 Mistakes That Destroy Your Charisma…and How to Avoid them'* and hope you find it informative.

Over the course of the book, you will gather information on what charisma is and the qualities that a charismatic person possesses. You will also gather information on what you should not do to destroy your charisma. It is important to remember that when one loses faith in you, it is hard to obtain that same level of trust. I hope the information in the book helps you stick to your beliefs and redefine yourself as a person.

Marilyn Monroe proved that one does not have to have an air about them to be charismatic. She was walking with a photographer and magazine editor towards the Grand Central Terminus deep in conversation. It was a busy day and the terminus was packed with people, and nobody had the time to look at her. As the photographer clicked the camera, she boarded the train and sat in the corner of a car.

Marilyn wanted to show the magazine editor that she could either choose to be plain Norma Jean Baker or glamorous Marilyn Monroe just by deciding. She was Norma Jean on the subway, but when she reached the sidewalks of New York, she chose to be Marilyn. She turned to the photographer and asked him if he would like to see Marilyn. All she did was turn around, fluff her hair and strike a pose, and she turned into the glamorous Marilyn Monroe.

A spark rippled out of her and she became magnetic. The people walking past her stopped in their tracks and recognized that a star was in their midst. In an instant, fans engulfed Marilyn and it took some time for the photographer to protect her from the crowd.

Charisma is a controversial and intriguing topic. People believe that charisma is a characteristic that people either have or do not have. There are some people who believe that charisma is often taken advantage of, while there are others who want to learn it. Regardless of how they feel about charisma, people are fascinated by it. Charismatic people have a significant impact on the world.

Have you ever wondered what it would be like to be as charismatic as Steve Jobs or Bill Clinton? Everybody has some charisma, but they can destroy it easily. Over the course of this book, you will gather information on what charisma is, and how people tend to destroy it. You will also learn what you should do to ensure that your actions do not destroy your charisma.

I hope you gather all the information that you are looking for.

Chapter One: What is Charisma?

People often struggle when they must define the word charisma. They find it especially hard to define the word in relation to social sciences and communication. Charisma is ultimately the result of good interpersonal and communication skills. Since one can learn to develop these skills, one can also learn to be charismatic.

How to be Charismatic

To become charismatic, you should pay attention to how you interact with people. A charismatic person has some qualities that appeal to others, and these qualities are all positive traits. They use their skills to attract people to them, and know what to say to ensure that people agree with them regardless of what the discussion is. It is for this reason that charisma is closely related to leadership skills, and it is important for a successful leader to be charismatic. Both Barack Obama and Bill Clinton are charismatic, and so are their wives. Their charisma helped them achieve success.

If someone asks you to think of a charismatic person, you will not think about yourself. You will first think about a celebrity, successful leader or a politician. It is true that their charisma led them to be successful, but there are many ordinary people who are charismatic. The staff at the restaurant making the most tips, the cool girl in school, the popular person in the office and the girl everybody wants to know, all have one thing in common – they are charismatic.

There are some people who are more charismatic when compared to others but, what makes you realize that someone is charismatic? Let us look at some of the characteristics of a charismatic person. Remember that you can develop these traits with ease.

Traits of a Charismatic Person

Self-Confidence

Charismatic people know how to appear confident, or are confident people. It is hard for most people to communicate or voice out their opinion when they are in a meeting, in a group, or speaking to an audience. A charismatic person knows how to communicate with people and helps other people also feel confident. This helps to enhance the process of communication. A charismatic person does not boast and is not egotistical. He or she is only confident about his values and beliefs.

Being Optimistic

Since a charismatic person is confident, he or she appears to also be optimistic. This means that they always try to see the best in a situation, event or in a person. They are often bubbly and cheery, and encourage people to be the best version of themselves. This helps people around them to have a positive outlook towards life.

An Emotional Player

To appear optimistic and confident, a person must act. Charismatic people can show their true emotions when they realize that their acting works in their favor. They also learn to mask their emotions and beliefs if they need someone to follow or agree with their beliefs. A charismatic player is like a swimming swan. He or she appears serene and calm on the surface, but there is a lot of internal activity that they hide from the public.

Being Interested and Interesting

Charismatic people know when they should listen to someone and when they want people to listen to them. They are good storytellers and know how to engage the crowd. They often communicate their messages concisely and clearly, and know when to be serious and when to inject humor in their conversation. They also know when to engage the audience, and how to ensure that the audience focuses on their speech.

Charismatic people know how to pay attention to the audience and will observe them to see what they can do better. If they are speaking to a small group or one person, they use relaxed and open body language while making eye contact. If they address a large group, they try to use their body language to let the audience know that they want to include everybody in the discussion.

They are often interested in others and ask questions to understand the opinions, feelings and views of other people. They do not have to extract information from people because they know how to make people feel at ease. People do not lie to them because they trust them to be open and honest. A charismatic person can sympathize and empathize with the people he or she speaks to and tries to remember details from previous conversations. This helps them build trust.

Maintaining eye contact, a simple smile, being courteous and polite are effective ways of making people understand your point. If you treat people well, they will be willing to do things for you.

Demonstrating and Being Intelligent

Since charismatic people want to communicate with people effectively, they know how to initiate a conversation with others. They often read and have sound knowledge about the current affairs and general knowledge. It makes it easier for them to make small talk with some people and move past the awkward beginning of the conversation.

Charismatic people are experts in some fields and know how to break complex concepts down in a way that helps their audience understand the concept. They also know how to change the explanation according to how the audience is receiving the information. This knowledge makes people trust charismatic people.

Being Assertive

Charismatic people know how to unite people over a common cause, or make them believe what they want them to. Most people use this ability for good causes, but there are others who use it to assert their right over others. Charismatic leaders can influence their followers and motivate people to do what they want. Some con artists are charismatic and they use their skills to gain respect and trust from their victims, and then they extort valuables and money from their victims.

It is hard to identify if a charismatic person is assertive since they are very subtle about it. They know what they should say to persuade people with words and emotions. They use their ability to understand their emotions and the emotions of the people around them, and use that knowledge to assert their beliefs.

Maintaining Attention to Detail

Charisma is about attention to detail. It also depends on interpersonal interactions. To be charismatic, you must learn to communicate effectively with enthusiasm and passion, while you display positive body language. You must think positively, be optimistic and display self-confidence. Charisma is also about building respect and about being persuasive whenever necessary.

You can be more charismatic by working on your interpersonal skills through practice. It is important to remember that you cannot please people all the time, regardless of how charismatic you are.

Chapter Two: How do People Destroy their Charisma?

When people work hard on their interpersonal skills, they become charismatic; however, some people destroy their charisma by being too mean or too proud of themselves. This chapter lists out the ten mistakes that people often make that destroy their charisma.

Never Introducing Themselves

Some people barge in on conversations and voice out their opinion. They forget that they should introduce themselves first and ask for permission to speak since they are not leading the discussion. For example, you can say, "Hi, I apologize for intruding, but I would like to introduce myself." That way, people know that you are polite and will include you in the conversation.

There are times when people are too shy and

avoid making eye contact with the people they are speaking to. When you do not look someone in the eye when you speak to them, you have lost them. They will not pay attention to you because they know you are not confident about what you are saying, and they will look for a way to get out of the conversation.

Not Introducing Your Friends or Guests

If you bring a friend to a party, you should ensure that you introduce that friend to the people at the party. Ensure that you do not shut your friends out. If you do not treat your inner circle well, you come across as being conceited and that you do not care for others. For example, if you are conversing with a group of friends, include your guests in the conversation by asking them what they think. If you do not make people feel welcome, they will stop hanging out with you.

Talking about Things that People do not Care About

You may love watching Anime or Sports, but some people may like to do the same thing. You can talk to them about it, but if you drone on and on about the same thing, boredom kicks in and people will want to leave the conversation.

You can tell people that you had a bad day at work, but if you give them every detail about your day, they will stop listening to you. You should ensure that you make the people around you comfortable and listen to what they have to say too. They should not leave the conversation with the impression that they wasted their time by listening to what you had to say about your life.

If you are running out of conversation starters, you can use some of the topics mentioned in the book, '*Shyness: 66 Easy Conversation Topics You Can Use to Talk to ANYONE.*'

Never Taking Feedback

You must pay attention to the audience and see how they react to a specific topic. When you see that people have not reacted to something you have said, you should stop and ask them a question to understand their views better. If the conversation does not shift back to what you were initially saying, you should take a hint and not go back to that topic. There is a possibility that people were zoning you out. When you do not take feedback into account, you show the people around you that their opinions do not matter. This turns people off and they may never want to speak with you again. You should also give feedback when someone else is talking.

Judging Others

It is not enough to have the confidence to show people your true personality. You should also learn to accept people for who they are. You cannot judge someone regardless of where they live, their occupation or where they come from. You must never let prejudice control your emotions. If you have read 'Pride and Prejudice,' you will remember that Elizabeth rejected Darcy's advances because she knew that he condemned others for being who they were. He also judged their circumstances. This is not the type of person you want to be.

Mumbling

A charismatic person exudes confidence. He or she knows what they are saying and knows how to convince people that they are right. If you begin to mumble or constantly stutter, people will lose interest in your conversation. You must ensure that you are loud and confident about whatever you are saying. You need to keep the people engaged and hooked to your conversation.

Giving One-Word Answers

Never give people one-word answers because they ask you a question to understand your opinion. If they ask you a question about the weather, you do not have to give them an elaborate answer about how you feel but, if they ask you about something on the news or about a holiday, do not give them one-word answers. You should try to elaborate and explain to them why you feel a specific way. When answering about the holiday, you can tell them about what you did and the places you visited.

Whining or Complaining

It is true that life is not as easy as people make it out to be. Even the most successful people have trouble in life but, do they whine? Do you think you can sort the problem out if you constantly whine or complain about how life is for you?

You can mention that there is an issue that is troubling you, but you cannot talk about it constantly. Nobody likes people who complain, and I am sure you do not like them too. If you constantly complain to another person, you are being a hypocrite.

As Bob Marley said, "When you worry, you make it double." Many studies concluded that people who often complained were lazy. They also took it upon themselves to bring their friends down with them. It is important to remember that there is nothing more unattractive than a person who does not want to do well in life.

Never Remembering Names

When you are talking to someone, you should remember his or her name. You can use the Dale Carnegie method and repeat their name back to them. If you still do not remember their name, you can ask them to spell it out for you. It is rude to forget someone's name and expect them to listen to your conversation. You should avoid repeating their name constantly because that is a sign of submission.

Lacking Ideas and Principles

Everybody has insecurities because there is massive pressure to fit in. People often hide their true beliefs and principles because they worry that those beliefs will brand them as being weird but, when you lack principle, people will not remember you. Can you name any public figure who has no principles? I bet you cannot name even one. These principles do not always have to be right.

You must ensure that you are always true to yourself and do not succumb to others' expectations of you. People who stand out are given respect because they stick to their character regardless of what the situation may be.

Chapter Three: How to Improve Charisma

We often forget to live in the present and worry about what the future will look like for us. This can affect us in many ways, and one of the effects of not living in the present is that you lose your charisma. If you partially listen to what someone says or ignore them, you cannot charm them.

There are many tips that you can use to improve charisma, but the most important thing you must do is focus on your mental state. You must improve the connection between your mind and body. This chapter provides three exercises that you can use to improve that connection. You will find that you can have great conversations within no time.

Always be Present in Any Conversation

Human beings hate uncertainty. Multiple

surveys show that human beings will prefer to hear bad news than not know what the outcome of a situation is. Go back to a time when you were head over heels in love with someone. How did you feel when that person stopped responding to your calls and messages? You thought it was over, but you did not know for sure. So, what did you do? You held onto that uncertainty for days, weeks and months. People will notice the change in your behavior. This change will affect your other relationships too. When you are uncertain, you often stop focusing on the present.

To fix this, you must note when your thoughts begin to wander when you are talking to someone. You may think that the other person will not notice, but you are wrong on most occasions. Your expressions will let the person know that you have phased out of the conversation, and you cannot answer a question if he or she wants to know what you think. This will ruin your charisma.

When you notice that your mind has started to wander, you should start to focus on your breathing. When your mind comes back, pay attention to what the person is talking about. Another technique that you can use is to focus on how your toes feel. You can pull your mind back and make it focus on one spot. This will make it easier for you to shift to the current conversation.

Lighten Your Load

When you are highly stressed, it will affect your social skills. There are some people who enjoy telling others how busy they are and talk about what a rush they are in. This will buy them attention for a small period, but the people who remain calm and cool are the ones who win the battle. You must remember that people love it when another person makes them feel at ease.

To bring yourself to this state, perform the

following exercise before you meet someone:

- Take five minutes and sit down in a calm spot in your house.

- Imagine the issues that are stressing you out.

- Now, visualize that you have given up on these tasks and asked somebody else to take care of them temporarily. It can be your friend, colleague or even the Universe. This may sound easy, but it is hard to do.

When you perform this exercise, you will feel better and will find that you can participate in conversations freely. You will also encourage the people around you to let their guard down.

Make them Feel Like a Star

Most amateurs know what it takes to look smart but, people who have exceptional interpersonal and social skills know how they can make other people the star of the conversation. When you talk to someone, you should avoid bragging about yourself, because that comes off as trying too hard to make an impression. This is when the other person knows you are insecure about who you are. Instead of focusing on yourself, ask the other person about them and make them feel good about themselves.

You can only be this way if you have practiced. You must strike the right balance between being charming and sucking up to someone. When you identify the right mix, people will want to be with you. You can become a dynamic speaker and work with people around you in a way you never have before. Remember that you are successful when you can make the people around you feel good about themselves.

Other Tips

Use Metaphors

You can use metaphors when you talk about your group. This group can be a sports team or an army. Lady Gaga refers to her fans as "Little Monsters." When Prince slapped the word "slave" across his face and appeared on television, he invoked a very powerful metaphor. Charismatic people use metaphors since it helps them stir a person's imagination and emotions.

Use Anecdotes and Stories

It is important to use stories and anecdotes when you talk about your successes and failures. You can tell people a story of how you failed and what you did to overcome that failure. Many rock stars use these failures to establish a connection with their audience and their music. For example, Paul McCartney always started off with an anecdote when he sang a song he had written about someone. He would tell the audience a little story about the person before he performed.

Moral Conviction

As mentioned earlier, it is important that you stick to your beliefs and opinions. When you are confident about your beliefs, you appeal to people. When you tell people that they have to do the right thing, you indicate to them that you stick to your values. Many rock stars displayed moral conviction, and this helped them strengthen their bond with the audience. U2 had their fans marching around the stage when Aung San Suu was arrested. To support the Russian group that was imprisoned, Madonna printed the words "Pussy Riot" on her back.

Express Shared Feelings

If you feel the same way as another person, you should express that emotion. This expression helps to increase and strengthen the bond between the two of you. When you say, "I am excited about this opportunity," or "I am as overwhelmed as you are," you strengthen your connection.

Make Your Presence Known

You must let the people in the room know that you have arrived. You can only do this if you know how to carry yourself. When you watched Barack Obama give his speeches, you saw how the crowd kept quiet the minute he stepped onto the stage. This should be you if you want to be charismatic. The people you speak to should give you their time and listen to you. They should not interrupt you; however, these people should not be afraid of you. You should also give them the freedom to voice out their opinion and stick to their beliefs whenever necessary. People do not like the idea of a "Yes" man.

You can practice your walk, your gestures and your body language, before you enter a room.

This will help you maintain your cool and help you grasp the attention of the crowd.

Conclusion

Thank you for purchasing this book.

Charismatic people can grasp the attention of the people in the room when they enter the room or start talking. They can change the way people view them and build stronger relationships with people. Using their charm and wit, they can ensure that people trust their decisions and opinions. They do not use their charm or their power to make people do the wrong thing.

However, there are some people who lose their charisma or destroy it because they start to behave differently. For instance, too much stress can make people worry or wonder about what their day will look like tomorrow. What they forget is that people do not like it if others ignore them. It is small gestures like these that affect your charisma.